smart girl's GUIDE™

# GETTING IT TOGETHER

how to organize your space, your stuff,
your time—and your life

by Erin Falligant
illustrated by Brenna Vaughan

**Published by American Girl Publishing**

No part of this book may be used or reproduced in any manner whatsoever without written permission except in the case of brief quotations embodied in critical articles and reviews.

18 19 20 21 22 23 24 QP 10 9 8 7 6 5 4 3 2 1

Editorial Development: Darcie Johnston
Art Direction and Design: Dan Nordskog
Illustrations: Brenna Vaughan
Production: Jeannette Bailey, Teresa Belk, Caryl Boyer, Kristi Lively, Cynthia Stiles

**Library of Congress Cataloging-in-Publication Data**
Names: Falligant, Erin, author. | Vaughan, Brenna, illustrator.
Title: A smart girl's guide, getting it together : how to organize your space, your stuff, your time—and your life / by Erin Falligant ; illustrated by Brenna Vaughan.
Description: Middleton, WI : American Girl, 2017. |
Series: A smart girl's guide | Audience: Age: 10+
Identifiers: LCCN 2016024953 (print) | LCCN 2016037444 (ebook) |
ISBN 9781609588885 (pbk.) | ISBN 9781683370024 (ebook) | ISBN 9781683370024 (epub)
Subjects: LCSH: Time management—Juvenile literature. | Organization—Juvenile literature.
Classification: LCC HD69.T54 F35 2017 (print) | LCC HD69.T54 (ebook) |
DDC 646.700835/2—dc23
LC record available at https://lccn.loc.gov/2016024953

americangirl.com/service

# Dear Reader,

How did this book end up in your hands? Maybe you saw the cover and decided it was time to get it together. Maybe you're already organized but want to stay that way. Or maybe your parents secretly slipped the book into your backpack *(hint, hint)*. Whichever is true, this book's for you.

We all need help getting organized—even adults. Why? Because most of us were never taught how to do it. The good news is, organization is like any other skill. You can learn how to take control of your space and time. When you do, you'll feel a lot less stress—and you'll have more room in your life for what matters most to you.

But don't take our word for it. Read on to hear from other girls who found great ways to get it together. Try tips for organizing any space, from backpacks to bedrooms. Plan an extreme locker makeover, redesign your bedroom into mini rooms, and create space and storage for all your stuff. Get in better touch with time, too, and practice saying no to activities that *squeeeze* your schedule.

Sound overwhelming? Take a peek at the "One Small Step" ideas throughout the book. If all you do is breeze through and take those small steps, you'll feel more on top of everything in your life. And that will feel good—so good you may want to read on!

Ready to get started?

## Your friends at American Girl

# contents

# in the zone . . . . . . . . . 42

# about time . . . . . . . . . . 64

# schedule smarts . . . . . 82

MONDAY
| 6:30 | Prep for day |
| 10:00 | Book Report Due ★ |
| 12:00 | Lunch ♡ |
| 4:00 | BB Practice |
| 5:30 | Dinner |
| 6:30 | Chores |
| 7:00 | Homework |
| 9:00 | Bedtime ☾ |

# falling apart?

# a disorganized day

Have you ever had a day like this?

**7:07 a.m.**
You wake up late—again. The bus is coming in 20 minutes, and you still have homework to do!

**7:27 a.m.**
The bus comes . . . and goes. Where are you? In your closet, searching for a shoe.

**7:52 a.m.**
Mom (who's mad) drops you off at school. You whip open your locker and get buried in an avalanche of papers.

**7:56 a.m.**
You're late to math. At least you finished your homework. But wait! It's still at home on the kitchen counter!

**9:55 a.m.**
Your stomach is growling. Too bad you didn't have time for breakfast.

**11:17 a.m.**
Time for gym. Where are your gym shoes? Oops! You forgot those, too.

**1:45 p.m.**
Ugh. Science test! How were you supposed to study on top of your other homework?

**3:32 p.m.**
Whew! You're finally home. You'll do homework right away—after a snack And some time online.

**4:55 p.m.**
Dad's here to take you to dance practice! Already??? You race to your room to get changed.

**7:20 p.m.**
How can you do homework while your sister is watching your favorite movie? Hey, here's an idea! You'll get up early tomorrow and do homework then.

**9:21 p.m.**
As you drift off to sleep, you remember the bake sale. Tomorrow. You're supposed to bring a dozen cupcakes . . .

## Yikes! What a day!
Was it bad luck?
No.
Are you a bad student?
No.
Lazy?
Nope.
Try **disorganized.**

When you're disorganized, your space gets cluttered and you can't find what you need. You're late. You forget things. You're always stressed out and frustrated—and your parents and teachers (and friends and siblings and pets . . . ) might be getting frustrated with you, too.

Here's the good news: You can teach yourself tricks for staying on top of your stuff and your schedule. And when you start, you'll have more *yay!* days than *yikes!* days. You'll feel more relaxed. You'll laugh more and worry less. You'll be taking charge of your life—and that's one of the best feelings of all.

# what trips you up?

Maybe you keep a tidy room but can't keep track of time. Maybe you hate being late, but you don't mind dust bunnies—and books and sweaters and papers and markers and hair clips and socks—stuffed under your bed. Which of these sound like you?

I finished my homework—honest! I just can't remember where I put it.

Mornings are so hectic! I'm already stressed out by the time I get to school.

I'd make my bed, except then I'd have to find someplace to put my clothes. And my stuffed animals. And my books.

Sometimes I'm surprised by tests at school. How come no one else seems to be?

Are those clothes on the floor clean or dirty? It's hard to tell.

I keep my alarm clock by my bed so I can hit "snooze" in my sleep.

My backpack might weigh more than I do. I'm not exactly sure what's in there.

My reasons for not doing homework are more creative than my actual work.

Okay, I admit it. I once found moldy food in my backpack. Okay, twice . . .

I've gotten a bad grade because of a missed assignment or two . . . or three.

I forget my lunch, homework, or sports stuff at least once a week. Thank goodness my parents are just a phone call away.

Put things off till the last minute? Who, me?

Do homework in my bedroom? No way. My brain shuts down with all the clutter in there.

I totally forgot about my science project. Mom and I stayed up late to get it done, but I think the glue's still wet.

I finally found my missing book report! Crumpled up at the bottom of my backpack. At the end of the school year. *Sigh.*

I need a personal secretary to manage my crazy schedule.

A girl could trip and sprain her ankle walking across my room.

Who needs a calendar? My parents keep track of my schedule for me.

There's at least one drawer in my room that's too full to close.

Running late is one of my best forms of exercise.

# Answers

If you chose **mostly blue,** your stuff is tripping you up! But you can cut the clutter and take control of your space. Read the "At School" section of this book for tips on cleaning out your backpack and giving your locker a makeover. Then read on for fun ways to redo your room so that you can find what you need, when you need it—and love being there.

If you chose **mostly purple,** it's time to get in touch with time. Read the "About Time" section for ways to make friends with clocks and calendars. Practice tracking time while you're getting ready in the morning or doing homework at night. Once you figure out where your time is going, you can save it for the things that matter most to you.

If you chose **both colors,** you're like many girls (and a lot of adults). But not to worry. You can get it together, one step at a time. Read the "One Small Step" ideas in every section for quick, easy ways to cut clutter and take charge of your schedule. Those small steps will give you the confidence to make bigger changes later on.

# 7 reasons to get it together

Sure, getting organized takes a little time and work. But it's worth it! Here's why.

**1.** You'll save yourself loads of time later on—time you used to spend searching for things under your bed or at the bottom of your backpack.

**2.** You'll feel good being in your room, and you'll be proud to show it off to friends.

**3.** You'll argue less with your parents about things like getting homework done and being on time.

**4.** Instead of waking up in a panic, you'll wake up feeling calm and peaceful.

**5.** Your teachers will notice that something's up with you. You might even get better grades!

**6.** You'll have more time for the things you really want to do.

**7.** You'll feel in control of your life and ready to tackle **ANYTHING!**

# we did it!

Here are some ways that girls like you have found to manage their stuff, their space, and their schedule.

> Every time my school binder gets full, I clean it out. I look at every paper and ask, "Do I NEED this for my learning?" If not, I recycle it. My binder is much lighter now.
> —Nina

> I put labels on all my drawers so I always have specific places to put everything. My room is so much cleaner and more organized!
> —Bethany

> I used to be in a rush in the morning. Then I found out it works really well to lay out my clothes, put my homework in my backpack, and make my lunch the night before. When I get up, I'm all ready to go.
> —Makenna

> I write everything I need to do on a sticky note. It's a friendly little list.
> —Chloe

Because I forget EVERYTHING, I write a to-do list in a small notebook that I carry around, even at school. This makes me feel amazing! I know I can relax without worrying I forgot something.
—Maddy

I started setting my alarm clock 10 minutes earlier, and it made my mornings go sooo much smoother.
—Gracie

I use a big whiteboard for my schedule, homework, and any other info I need to know. It makes me feel like I have all my thoughts together.
—Caitlyn

I do my homework as soon as possible because it makes my evenings more calm and relaxed.
—Flo

I organized my whole room lately, and that made me feel REALLY fantastic!!!
—Abby

15

# at school

# backpack basics

Imagine it's a new school year. You're carrying a brand-new backpack with clean pockets and that new-backpack smell. It weighs next to nothing, and you can reach way down to the bottom. No wadded papers, no broken pencils, no crumbs.

Now imagine you can keep your backpack like that all year (okay, not the new-backpack smell). Backpacks are small spaces, right? That means they're easier than lockers and bedrooms to keep clutter-free, and they'll give you practice for tackling larger spaces later on.

You can de-clutter your backpack in three steps:

1. sort your stuff

2. put it away

3. keep it that way

To sort your backpack, you first need to see what's in there. So pick a night after school, take a deep breath, and dump everything out. Shake out every last pencil, penny, shred of paper, and morsel of food. Empty? Good. Now think about what belongs in your pack and what honestly doesn't.

## What belongs

- books, notebooks, and folders that you need for tonight's homework

- your assignment notebook or planner

- permission slips that need to be signed or returned to your teacher

- today's lunch containers and leftovers

- a few school supplies

- personal stuff you used today, such as gym shoes or your flute

## What doesn't

- the quiz you got back last Friday

- books for those blissful classes that gave no homework today

- extra school supplies (19 pencils? really?)

- your sweaty kneepads from volleyball practice three days ago

- all the torn, crumpled-up, dog-eared papers that you don't know what to do with

## One small step

Weigh your backpack. A disorganized backpack is usually a heavy backpack, which could hurt your neck, back, or shoulders. What's too heavy? More than 10 percent of your body weight. If you weigh 80 pounds, your backpack shouldn't weigh more than 8 pounds. If it's too heavy, challenge yourself to make it weigh less tomorrow.

# paper trails

Paper can be tough to sort. It's hard to know what to hang on to and what to let go of—and more of it just keeps coming! For every scrap of paper you find in your backpack, ask yourself . . .

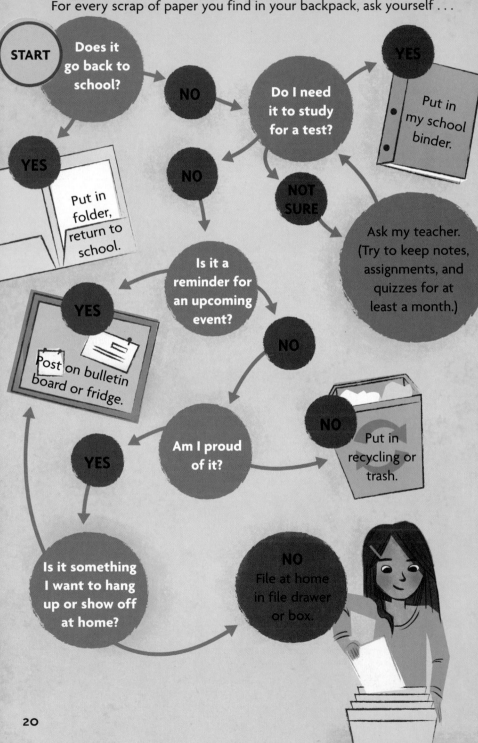

**START** — Does it go back to school?

**NO** → Do I need it to study for a test?

**YES** → Put in my school binder.

**NOT SURE** → Ask my teacher. (Try to keep notes, assignments, and quizzes for at least a month.)

**YES** → Put in folder, return to school.

**NO** → Is it a reminder for an upcoming event?

**YES** → Post on bulletin board or fridge.

**NO** → Am I proud of it?

**NO** → Put in recycling or trash.

**YES** → Is it something I want to hang up or show off at home?

**YES** → Post on bulletin board or fridge.

**NO** → File at home in file drawer or box.

# . . . and tamers

## Pocket folders

- Each subject gets its own folder. Pick colors you can easily remember, like a leafy-green folder for science.

- Use a separate folder for permission slips, lunch menus, and other non-homework papers.

- The left side of each folder is for homework you still have to do or permission slips that need to be signed. Move them to the right side when they're done or signed.

## One big binder

- Choose rings no wider than 1½ inches so it won't weigh you down.

- Keep subjects separate with colored divider tabs. Match the tabs to the colors you chose for your pocket folders so you don't have to think too hard.

- Put a pocket page after each tab to catch loose papers until you hole-punch them.

- Use plastic sleeves to protect anything you flip to a lot, such as your school schedule.

If papers are constantly spilling out of your binder, talk to your teachers and parents about using an accordion file folder or a binder that zips shut.

## File drawer at home

- Set up hanging folders, one for each subject. Add other folders for your awards, artwork and papers that you're proud of, and mementos that you want to keep.

- File boxes are great for more permanent storage or for when you don't have a file drawer. Label them on the front so you can easily see what's inside them.

## One small step

Go on a hunt for loose papers. Are they peeking out of your textbooks? Spilling out of your binder? Balled at the bottom of your backpack? Round them up and take care of them today.

# repack the pack

After you've unpacked your backpack and sorted your papers, it's time to reload. Follow this one simple rule: Pack only what you'll need today—or tomorrow, if you've got it together enough to pack the night before. Store everything else at school or at home.

## Pick a pocket

Put heavy books, binders, and lunch bags in the back pocket, closer to your body. They're easier to carry that way.

Fill the zippered pocket in front with small necessities (key, phone, $$). To save time, make a packing list and slide it into the front pocket or post it where you keep your pack. Then every morning, just check your list and go.

Put your pencil pouch, sweatshirt, and other light things in the middle pocket, if you have one.

If you have a side pocket for a water bottle, use it.

## Contain and clip

To keep tiny things from getting tossed around, try these tricks.

- Secure your library card, school ID, and lunch money with a binder clip.

- Keep the cord of your ear buds tangle-free by wrapping it around a clothespin.

- Slide hair elastics onto a carabiner, along with your house key.

- Tuck bobby pins, lip balm, and barrettes into a cleaned-out candy tin.

# keep it clean

The hard part's over! Here are some easy guidelines for staying on top of your pack so it never weighs you down again.

## 2 minutes

After school, every day, take 2 minutes to clean out your backpack. Toss trash. Rinse lunch containers. Put homework in a pile and permission slips on the counter for your parents to sign. And put away clothes and sports gear that you won't need tomorrow. (*Psst:* Put dirty clothes in the laundry so you'll have them when you need them next time.)

## 10 minutes

Every weekend, take 10 minutes to sort your pack. Are your pencils multiplying? Put some away in your desk and sharpen the rest. Is your binder getting heavy? Move worksheets or quizzes that are more than a month old into your file box or drawer, or recycle them if you're sure you're done with them. Is your backpack starting to smell like a gym locker? Ask your parents if you can throw it in the wash.

## Backpack bliss

Eventually, cleaning out your backpack will become a habit. You'll automatically start doing it after school, and you'll keep doing it.

Why? Because you'll love that you don't need a crane to lift your backpack. That you don't lose things in the black hole at the bottom. That you always have what you need, and know exactly which pocket to find it in. The time you spend sorting your pack equals the time you get back in the end—with fewer headaches, backaches, and stress.

# extreme locker makeover

Which school locker looks more like yours?
(Be honest!) If you answered **Before**...
you're due for a locker makeover!

# love your locker

A cluttered locker slows you down between classes and makes it hard to grab what you need at the end of the day. But you can pull it together. Start by sorting your stuff, then make a plan for where to put it.

## Pack it up

Take an empty cloth bag or two to school on Friday, and pack up anything you won't need next week. Bring home . . .

- the winter boots you haven't needed for two months.
- the six tubes of lip balm rolling around on the top shelf.
- pens, glue sticks, and other supplies that don't have a home.
- your Ancient Rome diorama from last quarter.
- loose papers and trash.
- notes, paper scraps, and magnets littering the inside of the locker door.
- dirty, crusty lunch containers.

## Sort it out

At home, empty the bags and take a good look at your stuff.

- Toss the trash.
- Stack loose papers in a pile, and use the tips from pages 20–21 to put them where they belong.
- Put gym clothes or sweatshirts in the hamper.
- Gather school supplies in one pile and toiletries in another, and decide what you really need at school and what can stay home.

# Make a plan

Once you know what you're taking back to school, think about what needs to . . .

- hang on a hook, such as your backpack and coat. If you don't have enough, buy extra magnetic ones. (Schools may not allow sticky ones.)

- be shelved, such as books and folders. Ask your parents (and school) if you can buy an extra locker shelf. Then put stuff for morning classes up top and afternoon classes below. Easy peasy.

- sit at the bottom, such as shoes or sports gear. Bring in a plastic bin with a lid or stacking drawers. (Measure your locker before you buy to make sure they fit.)

- adorn the inside of the door, such as a magnetic mirror and a dry-erase memo board, which can replace all the paper scraps and sticky notes.

- be contained, like pencils and lip balm. Buy a hanging locker organizer or use something from home, such as a travel toiletry bag or a pencil pouch.

- be thrown out. Hang a gift bag that can double as a trash bag.

## Got a locker mate?

Talk to her before doing any redesigning. Agree on a plan, and then inspire each other to keep things clutter-free.

## One small step

Draw a picture of your ideal locker. Sometimes having a picture in your mind of how organized your locker could be is the first step to making it happen.

# put away your gear

Now that you know where your locker loot goes,
put it away—and keep it that way.

## On Monday

Get to school early so you can make over your
locker before first period. Invite your mom
or dad to come, too—especially if you have
a lot to carry or are putting in an extra shelf.

## Every day

Repack your backpack throughout
the day, putting homework materials in it
after each class, and your lunch containers,
too. At the end of the day, you can
just grab your jacket and go.

## On Friday

At the end of the week, do your clean routine. Take home any clutter
that crept into your locker—papers that fell to the bottom, the project
you got back from art class, the umbrella from the day it rained. You'll
thank yourself on Monday, when you can start the week fresh.

# the end of the year

Sure, your homework is done when the last report card comes home, but sometimes papers, projects, and supplies live on—in places where they shouldn't. Follow these dos and don'ts.

**Don't . . .** bring home stuff from your locker and toss it in the closet till next fall. There could be something you need in there (such as a book your friend lent you) or something growing in there (such as the crust from your last PB&J).

**Do . . .** sort your stuff as soon as you can.

**Don't . . .** save every single assignment.

**Do . . .** save one or two assignments from each class, like a short story you wrote about your BFF or a test you studied really hard for. Store them in a file drawer or box, in a folder labeled with the year and grade you were in.

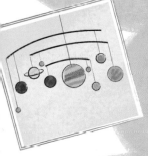

**Don't . . .** save every big project, like your three-foot model of the solar system or your craft-stick stegosaurus. Those just become more clutter to pick up or trip over.

**Do . . .** take a picture of projects before tossing or recycling them. A photo reminds you of your hard work but takes up a lot less space.

**Don't . . .** throw out all your folders and binders.

**Do . . .** save anything that's in good shape. Store school supplies where you and your family can use them all summer—and easily find them again next fall.

**Do . . .** enjoy your summer, now that you're clutter-free!

# at home

# clutter crisis

Do you have exactly zero space in your bedroom to do homework? Ever wonder whether the clothes on the floor are dirty or clean? Feel stressed out the second you step through the door? If you answered yes to any of these questions, odds are good that you're in clutter crisis.

## Clutter can . . .

- trip you up (sometimes literally—*ouch!*).
- slow you down (because you can't find what you need).
- sneak up on you (oozing out of closets or drawers).
- steal your treasures (because you can't see them behind all the other stuff).
- be hard to tame (like a wild animal).

But when you take control of clutter, everything changes. You can walk, work, sleep—and even breathe!—more easily in your room. Your space becomes your own again.

# what's clutter, really?

Take this quiz to find out. Which of these would you call clutter?

1. The learn-to-knit kit that you've had for two years but never opened. (Hey, you might want to learn someday . . . )

2. The posters plastered to your walls of bands you don't listen to anymore.

3. The maxi skirt your aunt bought for your birthday. Sure, it fits your body. You're just not sure it suits your style.

4. The purple flip-flops resting next to the lavender flip-flops piled on top of the magenta flip-flops.

5. The eraser collection that has spilled, crept, and leapt into every drawer of your desk.

6. Bow-Wow, the only stuffed animal you've had since you were a baby. He's missing an eye, but he still watches over you from his place on your pillow.

# Answers

**1. Clutter.** If you haven't been overtaken by the powerful urge to knit yet, let's face it: You probably never will be. Save that spot on your shelf for something you might enjoy more.

**2. Clutter.** You used to love these bands, but you've moved on. Your bedroom walls are valuable real estate. They should reflect what you love right now.

**3. Clutter.** If you keep everything that fits your body, your clothes may no longer fit your closet. Hanging on to gifts out of guilt can also lead to clutter. It's okay to let them go.

**4. Clutter.** We get it—you love flip-flops (and the color purple!). But if you have too many of the same thing, those cute accessories can clutter up your room.

**5. Clutter.** When the things you collect spill into lots of different spaces, they can start to stress you out.

**6. Not clutter.** How do you know? Because you still love Bow-Wow, you have only one Bow-Wow, and you keep your beloved Bow-Wow where you can see and cuddle with him every day.

The truth is, only you know which of your possessions you still use and still love. That means you can't hire someone to de-clutter your room for you *(sigh)*. But you can use what you know about yourself and your stuff to create a room you adore—a room that reflects who you are today.

# start smart

How is a bedroom like a backpack? You organize it the same way:
Sort your stuff, put it away, and keep it that way. How is a bedroom
not like a backpack? It's, um, bigger. Before you panic, remind yourself
why you're doing this: to love your room more and to stress less.
And you can get there quickly, if you start smart.

## Pick the right time.

Try the weekend, when you don't have
a gazillion things to run off and do.

## Pass through with a laundry basket.

Pick up anything that doesn't belong in your
room. The empty cereal bowl? Put it in the
basket. Dirty soccer ball? In the basket.
Wet bathroom towel? Basket, definitely.
Then take the items to where they belong.

## Unbury your bed— and then make it.

Need a forklift to remove the piles of
clothes, books, and stuffed animals? That's
all the more reason to get it done. Once
your bed is made, your room will instantly
look better. That'll give you the confidence
and energy to keep going—and, hey, you
might finally get a good night's sleep.

### One small step

Imagine how your room could
look. Tear out a picture from
a magazine or print something
you find online. If you know
how you want your room
to look, you have a better
shot at getting it there.

# sort your stuff

Your bed is made, and your room already looks better. It's time to sort your stuff, and you're eager (or at least willing) to dive in. But where do you begin? It's best to start with something easy.

## Easy to sort

- A small space, such as a desk drawer or a single shelf of books

- A hot spot where random things seem to collect, like under your bed or on your dresser

- A category of things, such as homework supplies or hair accessories. Do a clean sweep of your room to gather all of that "thing" before sorting.

## Harder to sort

- Stuffed animals, because you love them all, right?

- Collections, like snow globes or key chains

- Other sentimental stuff, like photos or souvenirs. If your bottom lip trembles even thinking about getting rid of some of this, save it for later—when you've developed some mad sorting skills.

## Ready to start?

**Step 1:** Set a timer for 15 minutes. If you want to quit after that, you can—really! Just try another 15 minutes later on.

**Step 2:** Turn on some dance music. Strut your stuff as you sort.

**Step 3:** Label three boxes or paper bags with the words **Keep, Toss,** and **Give Away.** As you sort, decide which box each item goes in and put it there.

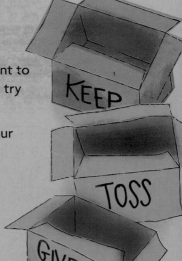

# Ask yourself these questions...

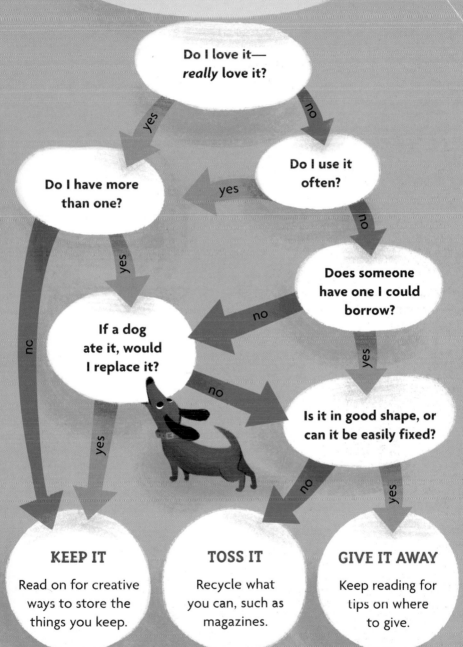

Do I love it—*really* love it?

yes → Do I have more than one?

no → Do I use it often?

yes → Do I have more than one?

no → Does someone have one I could borrow?

Do I have more than one?
- yes → If a dog ate it, would I replace it?
- no → KEEP IT

Does someone have one I could borrow?
- no → If a dog ate it, would I replace it?
- yes → Is it in good shape, or can it be easily fixed?

If a dog ate it, would I replace it?
- yes → KEEP IT
- no → Is it in good shape, or can it be easily fixed?

Is it in good shape, or can it be easily fixed?
- no → TOSS IT
- yes → GIVE IT AWAY

## KEEP IT
Read on for creative ways to store the things you keep.

## TOSS IT
Recycle what you can, such as magazines.

## GIVE IT AWAY
Keep reading for tips on where to give.

Always check with a parent before tossing something or giving it away. Your parents will probably be thrilled that you're cutting clutter, but ask first, just to be sure.

# going, going, gone

Parting with your things is much easier when you know they're going to good homes. Partner with a parent to donate your things or to convert your clutter into cash.

## Give . . .

- only items that are in good condition.

- clothes to homeless shelters or donation centers such as Goodwill, Salvation Army, Purple Heart, churches, and other organizations that help in your community.

- books to libraries and after-school programs.

- toys, dolls, and stuffed animals to younger relatives. (But don't donate everything to your little sister just because you can't bear to part with it. You might send her into clutter crisis, too!)

## Sell . . .

- media, such as movies and video games, at resale book-stores or game shops.

- sports equipment at resale sporting-goods stores.

- collectibles online. (Always have your parents post the items in their name and communicate with anyone who wants to buy them.)

- anything else that's in good shape at garage or thrift sales.

Once you've sorted your things and gotten rid of some clutter, give yourself a pat on the back—a *big* pat. Giving away your belongings is hard, but what you have left are things you truly want and love. You can find them more easily. You'll be able to see them better, which will make you smile when you walk into your room. And you may have given other girls something "new" to love, too.

## One small step

Can't let go of something you think you should? Ask a parent to hide it from you for a month (in a good spot— not the one you discovered last holiday season). If you completely forget about that thing, congratulations! You're ready to let go. If you really miss it, try sharing it with a sibling or friend so you can still have it part of the time. Call it "joint custody," and see if you can part with it for good during your next big sorting session.

# great giveaways

These girls gave something special away—and made someone else's day.

After my birthday party when I turned eight, my mom and I went to the hospital to donate all my gifts to the kids there. When I saw the kids' faces, it made my heart melt. It was one of the best experiences ever.
—Liz

When I was little, I had a movie that I watched all the time. I watched it less and less as I got older. My bus driver had a little girl, and I gave her the movie. I felt so happy afterward knowing she'll enjoy the same movie I grew up with!
—Kimi

When I was six, I gave away a stuffed bunny that I loved. Some people at church knew a family whose house had just burned down, and I sent my bunny to those kids. I missed my bunny, but I felt happy that they had a stuffed animal to keep them company.
—Emily

I had a dollhouse that was my most prized possession. As I got older, I didn't play with it as much. I gave it to a little girl at our church who had been wanting one. I was sad to say good-bye to my dollhouse, but it was worth it to see the smile on her face.
—Darra

I gave two bags of stuffed animals to a donation center. I realized there were kids out there who don't have a stuffed toy. Afterward I felt really good! It was hard to let go of some awesome childhood memories, but I knew that whoever received my toys would make *more* memories.
—Madison

I gave away a special bike. I don't know who got it, but I felt good afterward for giving a kid something that she might love.
—Cara

ENTERTAINMENT ZONE

# in the zone

CLOTHING ZONE

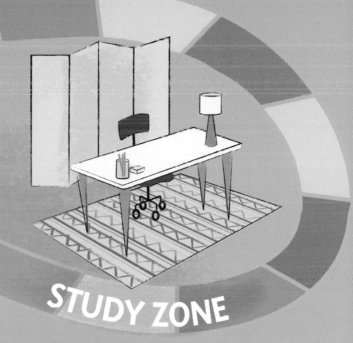

# STUDY ZONE

# GET READY ZONE

# SLEEP ZONE

# the five zones

Yay, you! You've sorted your things. You've given some away. And what you have left are the things you really love.

Now where's the best place to put everything? Think of your bedroom as a small apartment. You sleep there. You study. You get dressed and ready for school. You hang out with friends. There's a whole lot going on in that space! No wonder it feels cluttered and chaotic sometimes.

A simple way to tame your space and keep your cool is to create "mini rooms" for everything you do. You don't have to call in a construction crew. Just think about where you do what.

## 1. Study zone

This is where you do your homework, hop online, and are sometimes inspired to create great art (or just doodle during study breaks).

## 2. Entertainment zone

This is where you hang out when a friend comes over or you want to relax. Maybe it's a beanbag chair by your bookshelf. Or it's the cozy rug where you do yoga, play a game, listen to tunes, or stretch out with a magazine.

## 3. Clothing zone

"Um, isn't this called a closet?" you ask. Sure, that's part of it. But it also includes your dresser and laundry basket.

## 4. Get-ready zone

Here's where you fix your hair, put on jewelry . . . and take a last deep breath before heading out the door.

## 5. Sleep zone

That's your bed, and maybe a bedside table with books and a reading lamp. Clothes, clutter, gadgets, and homework should be banned from this zone. Period.

# study zone

You sit down and your brain instantly fires up, ready to work. You have everything you need within reach—pencils, paper, calculator, books. There are no distractions, so you finish your homework in record time. You're pretty sure you aced it, too. Hurrah! Now you can get out of the study zone and move on to other things.

Is that how homework feels for you? Probably not. But it could! Here are the keys to a stellar study zone:

It's in the **same place** every day, like your desk or a certain spot at the kitchen table. When you sit there, your brain and body know it's time to work—because you've made a habit of it.

You have **supplies close by.** They're in your desk drawer, or they're in a tote or basket that you store in your room and can easily grab.

There are **no distractions** (or at least not too many). You can't see a TV screen, your phone is silenced, and your family knows to leave you alone.

Is your study zone your bed? Consider rezoning. You don't want to feel sleepy while you work—or worse yet, train your brain to fire up in your **sleep zone,** where you should be winding down.

# stress-free desk

A clutter-free workspace equals a clear head—one that's ready to get down to business. To de-clutter your desk . . .

**1.** Clear off **the top.** Keep out only the supplies you use every day. Put a few (3, not 30) pens and pencils in a mug or jar. Add a bowl for sticky notes, erasers, and a brain toy, like a ball or lump of putty. Squeezing the ball might help your brain focus and keep the rest of your body from fidgeting.

**2.** Use hanging **file folders** to separate papers in the bottom drawer.

**3.** Use a **drawer organizer** or shoebox lids to separate supplies such as pencils, scissors, and your glue stick in the top drawer. Move knick-knacks, jewelry, lip gloss, and granola bars somewhere else (especially the granola bars).

**4.** Put art and project supplies in a **plastic bin.** Slide it under your bed or desk to keep your drawers free for supplies you use more often.

## Paper plus

Schedules, artwork, awards—oh my! Try not to litter in your study zone. Put paper . . .

on a **bulletin board,** if you want to see something often. Calendars, sports schedules, and inspiring notes go here. (Take them down as soon as they have "expired" to keep your board clutter-free.)

in **frames** on your wall—such as honors, awards, and art that you're proud of. When you're ready to showcase something else, file the masterpiece or put it in a portfolio with plastic sleeves.

in a **file drawer** in your desk or a file box. Label each hanging folder with a school subject. Add folders for clubs or teams you're a part of and for special notes. Then go through your files after each grading period to recycle what you no longer need.

## Ditto for digital

Hard drives and thumb drives get cluttered, too. Organize them just like you do your paper files. Make a folder for each class. Then add subfolders for "Notes," "Papers," and "Projects." Be specific when you name files ("Ancient Greece Essay" is better than "History Essay"), and number each draft. Whenever you sort paper files, sort your e-files, too. Delete rough drafts and notes for units you've finished.

## Study zone to-go

No desk? Create a to-go tote that holds supplies: scratch paper, calculator, pens and pencils, sticky notes, and so on. Use something sturdy, like a basket, box, or plastic bin. And don't leave a trail of stuff behind, or you could lose your "study anywhere" privileges (and your favorite pen).

## One small step

Decorate a box to keep in your room for recycling paper. Then do a quick pass through your room, and score two points for every paper ball you toss into the box.

# entertainment zone

Books and games, stuffed animals and souvenirs.
These are things that make you happy, right?
So make sure they're easy to see and store.

## Games, CDs, and DVDs

Stack board games on a shelf or in plastic crates. Store video games spine-out on a shelf. Do you own music or movies on disc? Store the cases in a box, and slide the discs into a binder with plastic sleeves. Just flip through to find the disc you want.

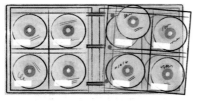

## Electronic devices

Store your phone, tablet, hand-held games, and chargers in a basket. Keep it near a power outlet away from your bed—because lit-up screens charge up your brain, making it hard to sleep. Or create a family device center where you all "check in" your devices at night.

## Books and magazines

Store magazines in a basket or in a magazine holder on your bookshelf. Of course, books go there, too!

## Floor space

Save floor space for playing games or for dancing, yoga, or just hanging out. Throw down a pretty rug. Add a beanbag chair or big pillow for sitting on.

## One small step

Play **hot lava.** Look around your entertainment zone and make sure no loose items are touching the floor. If they are, find them a new home in a box, bag, basket, or bin.

## Furry friends

You love your little buddies too much to give them away, but don't let them run wild. Shepherd them into a basket or a pet net hanging from the ceiling.

## Collections

Watch out! These spread like wildfire, too. Here's how to take control:

- Put everything in one place. Line up snow globes on a shelf, dangle a key chain collection from a jewelry tree, and slide postcards into a photo album.

- Display only what you love right now. Show off your newest collections or the ones you can't bear to tuck away. Store older collections in plastic bins or decorated, labeled shoeboxes.

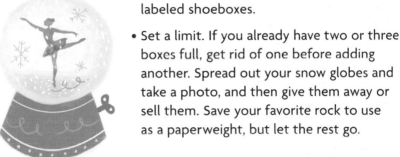

- Set a limit. If you already have two or three boxes full, get rid of one before adding another. Spread out your snow globes and take a photo, and then give them away or sell them. Save your favorite rock to use as a paperweight, but let the rest go.

## Photos and videos

Store printed photos in albums or photo boxes. Digital photos and videos? Those get cluttered, too. Sort them right away when you upload them to a computer. Delete bad shots and duplicates, and drag-and-drop your favorites into albums with titles like "holidays," "pets," "vacation," and "friends." Talk to your parents about backing up photos and videos regularly.

## Souvenirs and other special stuff

Tack some of what you love to your bulletin board. Store the rest in scrapbooks or acid-free photo boxes. When a book or box gets full, sort it—and save only what makes you smile.

# your shelve-it style

#### Which answers sound most like you?

**1.** You're looking for the book called *Birds Know Best*. You search your shelf . . .

   **a.** for the cover. You know it's canary yellow.

   **b.** for the title. It should be alphabetized right after *Birds and the Girls Who Love Them*.

   **c.** and then remember you were reading the book in bed. It must be on your nightstand.

**2.** You promised your friend you'd watch *Funniest Cat Videos Part 3* tonight. But when you open the DVD case, you find part 2. When you open the case for part 2, you find part 1. You decide to . . .

   **a.** open up every DVD case you own to see what you have.

   **b.** find part 3 so that you can put those three cases back in order on your shelf.

   **c.** watch part 1, because it's easiest to grab. Besides, if you've seen one cat video, you've seen them all . . .

**3.** When your collection of chickens starts to overtake your shelves, you . . .

   **a.** line them up on your desk and headboard, too, so that you can see every feathered face.

   **b.** decide which one is your most favorite, next favorite, and third favorite. Maybe you'll give the rest away.

   **c.** leave a few cute chicks on your middle shelf and put the others in a plastic bin on your top shelf.

**4.** When you want to try a hairstyle from last summer's *American Curl* magazine, you . . .

   **a.** pull out the green magazine from the rainbow of issues in your magazine holder.

   **b.** reach under the tall stack on your shelf. You keep the older ones near the bottom.

   **c.** hurry into the bathroom. You remember tearing out that page and keeping it with your hair clips.

**5.** Where's that photo of you and your sister surviving the Super-Duper-Loop-da-Looper roller coaster?

   **a.** In the middle of your bulletin board, of course.

   **b.** In a box on your shelf—you know which one.

   **c.** In a summer vacation scrapbook that you like to show your friends.

## Answers

If you answered **mostly a's,** you're a visual girl who can picture every book she owns and likes to store things where she can see them. Try creating a rainbow of books, with red and orange covers on top shelves and blue and purple on bottom shelves. Or store some of your favorite book covers face out, like works of art.

If you answered **mostly b's,** you're a sequential girl who likes to store things in order. That doesn't mean you're a neat freak. You're perfectly fine with piles, because you know exactly what's in them. Try alphabetizing your books by author or title. Move from A to Z (or from Z to A, if you want to be different).

If you answered **mostly c's,** you're a practical girl who likes to put things where you'll use them most. Try shelving your books by popularity, putting your favorite ones on the middle shelves, where they're easy to grab. Or fill those middle shelves with your favorite genre of books, such as fantasies, mysteries, or biographies.

Whichever style you choose, leave room to grow. Try to fill each shelf no more than two-thirds full.

# clothing zone

When you sorted your closet, did you discover hidden treasures? Maybe you found a sweater that had fallen from its hanger into a dark corner. Or a cute dress in the way, way back that still had a price tag dangling from it. If you can't see some of the clothes in your closet, you'll eventually forget you have them. What a waste! Organize your closet in a way that lets you see more. Try organizing . . .

## By style

Hang short-sleeved shirts together, sweaters with sweaters, pants with pants, and skirts with skirts. Just check the weather forecast, and you'll know exactly which part of your closet to turn to.

## By color

Create a rainbow from one end to the other. Start with reds and oranges and move toward blues and purples. Need a boost of confidence for team tryouts or that big test? Go for red. Feeling calm and cool on a Friday? Blue's the color for you.

## By season

If you can't find your sundresses because you have
too many sweaters, get those sweaters out of there.
Hang off-season clothes in the back of the closet, or tuck them in
a bin under your bed. (Aren't you glad you cleaned under your bed?)

## By size

Move from long to short. Hang pants and long skirts at one end
of your closet and shorter skirts and shirts at the other. See space
underneath those shorter clothes? Use it! Tuck a shoe rack there.

### Decide which system works best for you.

Then turn around and try something new. Why? Because organizing your
closet in a fresh way makes your clothes look fresh and new, too—no
shopping required!

## One small step

Do clean clothes rarely make it into
your closet? Maybe they magically
appear on your bed, nicely folded,
and there they stay. You sleep with
them, you work around them, and
eventually you're not sure what's
clean and what's dirty.

So try this: Ask a parent if you can
have two different-colored laundry
baskets—one for dirty and one for
clean. Clean clothes can stay in the
basket as long as you don't let them
creep onto the bed or the floor.

# Shoes and boots

Got a pile of 'em? If you find yourself choosing the first matching pair instead of digging for the shoes you want to wear, it's time to ditch the pile method. Instead, line up your shoes and boots in pairs so they're easy to find.

- Pair up shoes on a standing shoe rack or in an over-the-door shoe organizer.

- "File" your flip-flops and sandals in a magazine rack or mail organizer on your closet shelf.

- Stuff boots with tissue paper, or ask a parent if you can cut an old pool noodle to fit inside. That'll help them stand up straight and keep their shape.

# Accessories

Scarves, purses, belts, and baseball caps—you can hang only so many of them on your doorknob. You could spend money on fancy contraptions to hold them, or you could try the magic-ring trick. Put a row of shower-curtain rings on a hanger, and loop belt buckles and purse straps through them. It works for scarves and tank tops, too. Who knew?

## Sports gear

Is your gear here, there, and everywhere? Ask a parent about storing larger gear in another part of the house, such as the garage. For the rest, try these tricks: Stand up bats, lacrosse sticks, and rackets in tall laundry baskets or kitchen trash bins. Hang helmets from hooks on the wall. Gather balls in mesh laundry bags, and hang them from hooks, too.

## Socks and undies

Do you wear mismatched socks as a fashion statement—or because you can't find a matching pair? Try dividing up your sock and under-wear drawers using small fabric boxes, plastic totes or trays, or even shoeboxes cut to fit your drawer. You'll be searching for lost socks no more.

## Shorts and tees

Remember: If you can't see 'em, you won't wear 'em. So when you put clothes in a dresser drawer, don't pile them up. Instead, stack shorts and T-shirts as if you're putting them on a shelf, then turn them sideways in your drawer. (You may need to fold them smaller and tighter.) Can you see the edge of each one? That's the idea!

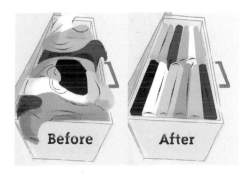

Before          After

55

# get-ready zone

This is where you get ready in the morning, sometimes in record time *(whew!)*. Do you have what you need there? Can you get in and out without stress or mess? Here's how to make the most of your get-ready zone.

## Mirror, mirror

Where do you take that last look before you dash out the door? Keep hair accessories and jewelry nearby.

Hang a shower caddy from the mirror, and store brushes and combs in it.

Dangle bracelets and necklaces from coat or sweater hooks on the wall near the mirror.

Press a suction-cup hook to the mirror, and hang a small gift bag to hold ponytail holders and headbands.

Use a suction-cup soap dish to store hair clips, rings, and other small things.

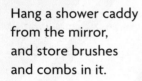

Tuck earrings, charms, and pendants into a colored ice-cube tray.

# De-stressed dresser

A clear dresser top helps keep your mind clear in the morning, too.

Use a pretty tray or place mat to protect the surface from leaky lotions and sprays.

Tuck small toiletries, like lip gloss and nail polish, inside stacking drawers or stackable plastic containers with lids.

Ask if you can cover your dresser with a clear acrylic sheet (cut to fit at hardware stores). Slide scrapbook paper, photos, and other mementos underneath.

## One small step

Move your messiest toiletries to the bathroom—or into a plastic tote that you carry to the bathroom each morning. You'll avoid gooping and gunking up your get-ready zone. And your parents will think you're brilliant!

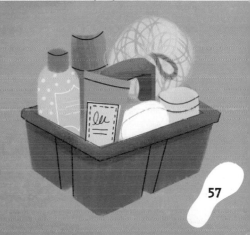

# shared zones

If you share a bedroom, setting up your zones is more complicated. But it's also more necessary, because there's twice as much stuff to keep track of. So get creative!

Share the mirror in your get-ready zone, but keep your things in separate plastic totes.

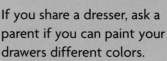

If you share a dresser, ask a parent if you can paint your drawers different colors.

Forget masking tape! To divide the room, arrange a pair of low bookshelves back-to-back, and anchor them together at the top for safety.

Your bed is your own, which means the space underneath it is, too. Try an under-the-bed bin on wheels for storing your things.

Pull a curtain when you want privacy for studying or if you have different bedtimes. Headphones, fans, and white noise machines can help make your study and sleep zones feel more private, too.

Try color-coded hangers: one color for your clothes and another for your sister's.

Don't share the study zone at the same time. Try different desks facing away from each other, or set up a second study zone in another part of the house.

59

# two homes

If you split time between two homes, your rooms won't be set up exactly the same way. It's fun to try out different looks and room arrangements, but if *everything* is different, it's hard to find what you need. (Did you forget to pack it, or is it just stored in a different place?)

You might struggle to fall asleep the first night back in one home. Or it might be hard to study, because your study zone isn't set up like it is in your other home. Here's how to stay sane, get your sleep (and study time), and feel at home in both homes.

## Double up

You don't want to lug around a 600-pound suitcase. And your parents don't love those late-night, panicky drives across town to get something you forgot. So try to have these things in both homes:

**Chargers** for your cell phone, computer, or tablet

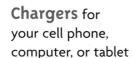

**School supplies**

**Underwear, socks, and pj's**

**Toiletries,** such as a toothbrush, toothpaste, shampoo, face wash, brush, and comb

**Comfy clothes,** like jeans, and some fancy clothes, too (because you never know when you'll be invited to a royal ball)

**Photos** of your parents. No matter how old you are, there are going to be times when you miss one parent or the other. Stay close with photos (and phone calls).

## List it

For the things you have to bring back and forth between homes, make a "Don't Forget" list to look at each time you make the switch.

Make a few copies of the list. Keep one in your duffel bag and your backpack, and post the others on the fridge in both homes.

DON'T-FORGET LIST

BACK PACK
· binder
· Planner
· pencil pouch
· homework!

GYM CLOTHES + SHOES
LACROSSE STUFF
PHONE
TABLET
FLUTE + MUSIC FOLDER
MY STUFFIE :)

## Study the same way

If you struggle to get homework done in one home, think about how your study zone is set up. Is it too noisy? Too quiet? Do you have the supplies you need? Are you studying at a different time of day? Remember habits: You train your brain to kick in by creating a routine and sticking to it. Talk to your parents about keeping your study routine as similar as possible in both homes.

## Park it

Choose a place to store your duffel at each home. That way, you and your parents can add things to it as soon as you remember you might need them at the other house. And you'll know exactly where to pick up your bag when it's time to go.

## Protect your ZZZs

When you sleep in a new place, whether it's a hotel room or a friend's house, it can be hard to drift off. Your body picks up on new sounds or different lighting. So keep your two sleep zones feeling similar. Bring the same pillow or blanket back and forth, if you can. Use a nightlight in both rooms so that one isn't darker than the other. Pack a book so you can read the same story every night. Needing those things doesn't mean you're a baby—it just means you're human. Your body is fighting sleep because it wants to keep you safe, so meet it halfway with a few comforting things.

# keep it clutter-free

You've cut clutter and created zones. You know exactly where everything is, and when you look around your room, it's filled with things that make you smile. Bravo! You're in control of your space. And you want to keep it that way, right? Here's how.

## Take a stroll.

Each night before bed, walk through your room and put things back where they belong. You'll sleep better if things are in their place (especially anything that was piled on your pillow or tossed on your bed), and tomorrow morning will feel less stressful, too. And if your parents ask why you're doing laps in your room? Tell them. You might inspire them to de-clutter as well!

## Set space limits.

You have only a certain number of hangers in your closet. You have a few bins under your bed and on your shelves. So when those are full, you go out and buy some more, right? Nope. If you do that, where will it end? Your room could start looking like a container store. So make this rule: When those hangers, boxes, and bins are full and you want to store something new, something else has to come out.

## Schedule sorts.

When is it time to sort again? For clothing, it's the end of each season. You're growing all the time, and styles are ever changing. So if you haven't worn something this season, you probably won't be thrilled to wear it next year at this time (and it probably won't fit). For school papers and stuff, schedule your sorting sessions at the end of each grading period or semester.

# Shop smart.

You're at the mall and you've got that thing in your hand that you think you really want. You're heading toward the checkout line. STOP. Now's a good time to picture your amazing room and to remember how hard you worked to rid it of things you didn't really love or need. Before you buy, ask yourself these familiar questions:

**Do I really need it?**

**Will I use it often?**

**Could I borrow one instead?**

**Do I really love it?**

**Do I already have one?**

It's hard to resist the urge to buy. Why? Because ads online, on TV, and in magazines want you to believe that you need to have *more*. But you already know better. You know that having more stuff just means more to take care of. More time spent organizing or trying to find what you need. More stress.

If you don't buy the thing that's burning in your hand right now, there's one thing you'll definitely have more of: money. And you can save that money for something that you really do love.

# Rethink wish lists.

The same goes for gifts. Having family members go in on one quality item can make more sense than getting lots of little things that just clutter your space and bore you within a week. So if you make holiday or birthday wish lists, ask for one or two things that you really want. Or ask for an experience, like a concert or a trip to a water park. Experiences will leave you with memories that take up no space at all.

## One small step

Before you buy something, wait a day or two. Sleep on it. Look around your room and think about where you'll put it. If you're still sure tomorrow that you love and want that thing, go ahead and buy it. If not, save your money. Remind yourself how hard you worked to create the bedroom you have today—and keep it that way.

# about time

# crunch time

Taking control of your time may feel tougher than organizing your stuff. Why? Because you can't see it! Unlike the clutter that spills out of closets and drawers, time is invisible. It can sneak up on you or fly right on by.

When do you struggle with time? To find out, choose all the answers that sound like you. (It's okay to choose more than one.)

**1.** You often holler "just a sec!" when you're . . .

  **a.** getting ready for school and your mom or dad is in the car, leaning on the horn.

  **b.** catching a few minutes of reality TV before facing the reality of your homework.

  **c.** scribbling one more answer on your test while your teacher is trying to slide it off your desk.

**2.** Which of these totally annoy you?

  **a.** The sound of your alarm clock.

  **b.** The *pew, pew, pew!* of your sibling's video game while you're trying to study.

  **c.** The words "So, have you started that big project yet?"

**3.** Your parents would think an alien had abducted your body if you . . .
   **a.** showed up early at the breakfast table, fully dressed.
   **b.** did your homework on Friday afternoon instead of
      Sunday night.
   **c.** finished your book report the day before it was due.

**4.** Your stomach talks to you . . .
   **a.** mid-morning, because you never have time
      for breakfast.
   **b.** right when you sit down to do homework.
      You jump up and grab a snack. And maybe
      another.
   **c.** when your teacher says it's test time. Yikes!
      Bring on the butterflies. If only you'd had more
      time to study.

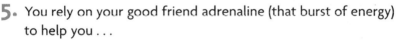

**5.** You rely on your good friend adrenaline (that burst of energy)
   to help you . . .
   **a.** catch your ride to school—you sometimes have to sprint.
   **b.** rush through your homework during breakfast.
   **c.** create a mind-blowing science project the night before it's due.

# Answers

If you chose **two or more a's,** your mornings are crunched for time. It feels *sooo* good to hit "snooze" and drift back to sleep. But running around like a maniac an hour later doesn't. If you start the morning stressed, that feeling's hard to shake—you end up racing from one thing to the next all day. So start smart by figuring out how much time you need to get ready, including eating a sit-down breakfast. Set your alarm to give yourself that time (plus a little extra), and swear off that risky snooze button.

If you chose **two or more b's,** study time stresses you out. Your mind and body start fighting you from the moment you sit down with your books. Everything takes longer than you think it's going to, especially with all the little breaks you seem to need. Set a timer and find ways to stick to your work, so you can push through study time in record time—and then move on to something way more fun.

If you chose **two or more c's,** you struggle with prepping for tests and long-term projects. Maybe you put them off because they're overwhelming (where do you even start?!) or because you underestimate how long they'll take to do. Either way, that night-before panic just isn't worth it. Even if by some miracle you get the work done, will you get a good grade on your last-minute work? Not likely. Figure out how to start early, and give yourself mini deadlines so that you're not racing the clock.

If you didn't choose two of any particular letter (and even left some questions unanswered because they just didn't sound like you), congratulations! When it comes to time management, you're a superhero. What planet are you from? We want to come visit—and get some tips!

# test of time

*Just a minute!* It's what we say when we want to buy more time. But how long is a minute really? Are you a good judge of time?

Test it out. Jot down how many minutes you think it takes you to do everyday things, such as . . .

- set the table.
- grab your favorite snack before starting homework.
- run for the school bus.
- get your backpack ready.
- get dressed in the morning.
- change into your pajamas and brush your teeth.
- read a chapter in your science book.
- eat a bowl of cereal.
- take a shower.

Now put your guesses to the test. Use a stopwatch or a kitchen timer to see how long each activity really takes. Any surprises?

Maybe something took a lot longer than you thought. Or maybe you finished these tasks in record time. Either way, you learned something. You learned that your time guess-timations may need tweaking—or that you really **kick it in** when you're on the clock. Figuring out how long it takes to do everyday routines is the first step toward making sure you leave enough time for them.

# morning madness

If morning is your crunch time, try these tips
for a smoother start to the day.

## List it.

Write down everything you do from the time you get up to the time
you leave for school. Then time yourself to see how long each step
takes. Don't rush. Maybe you're in speed mode today, but can you
do that every morning? And do you really want to? Be honest and
write down real numbers. Your list might look like this:

## Do the math.

Add up all that time and ask yourself, *Am I allowing enough time to get
these things done?* If your routine takes an hour and you get up only 45
minutes before the bus comes, it's easy to see why you feel frantic. Try
setting your alarm 10 or 15 minutes earlier. Your body may not miss those
few minutes of sleep, but they might help ease your morning. If you still
feel rushed, set your alarm back another 5 minutes the next day.

If you're already skimping on sleep, try another solution: Do parts of
your routine the night before. Packing a lunch, picking out clothes to
wear—can you move those things to evening instead? You might be
able to turn morning madness into something a lot more manageable.

# Beware of time stealers.

Do you get sucked into a TV show when you should be washing out your cereal bowl? Or find yourself in a cuddle fest with your cat, Boots, when you're supposed to be getting dressed? Those aren't bad things if they make your mornings sweeter. But they take time, so plan ahead for them. Or schedule an extra 10 minutes every morning to spend doing whatever you (and Boots) would like.

# One small step

You snooze, you lose—precious time, that is. Try moving your alarm clock across the room so you can't hit the snooze button in your sleep. An added bonus? As you cross the floor to shut off the alarm, your body will naturally start waking up. On the other hand, if you're groggy enough to sleep through that alarm, make sure you're getting enough sleep. Aim for 9 to 10 hours a night.

# study-time stress

You just got home from school. Your brain is drained. The last thing you feel like doing is studying. But if you put it off too long, it takes over your night. Don't let it! Here's how to make short work of homework.

## Schedule it.

When do you work best? Right after school? After a snack? After dinner? Try different times to see when you feel most alert. Then try to stick to the same time every day. Just don't push home-work too close to bedtime. Leave at least a half hour to let your brain wind down, or you'll be lying wide awake in bed—or having dreams about geometry.

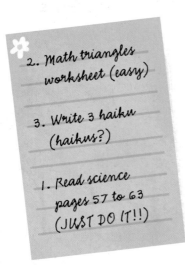

2. Math triangles worksheet (easy)

3. Write 3 haiku (haikus?)

1. Read science pages 57 to 63 (JUST DO IT!!)

## Put it in order.

Write down tonight's assignments, and then decide what order you'll do them in. Do you want to start with something easy so you can cross it off your list? Good choice. Do you want to start with the hardest thing first to get it over with? Another good choice. Choose whichever system helps you dive in and get started.

## Take a pop quiz.

Challenge yourself: How long do you think each assignment will take? Write down your guesses, and then time yourself as you work. Do this often enough, and two things will magically happen:

**Magic Thing 1:** You'll start getting better at judging time.

**Magic Thing 2:** You might focus better, trying to beat the clock.

Tap into your competitive streak, and connect with that girl inside who wants to win. Let her! You might win back some free time, too.

# Take mini breaks.

You need them—breaks for stretching, snacking, clearing your head, and resting your eyes. Use a timer to help you take a 5-minute break after every 20 minutes of studying. Hungry? Grab brain food, like fruit or crackers and cheese—something quick and not too messy. Stiff or twitchy? Take a few deep breaths and do some stretches, or blast a song and dance your heart out. Feeling social? Check your phone or snuggle with your dog. Make the most of those 5 minutes, and when the timer says your break is over, dive back into your work.

## One small step

If you're not ready to be "on the clock," at least keep one (a clock, that is) near your study zone. Analog clocks and watches, which have hands that move rather than digital numbers, work best because they show you chunks of time. And like slices of your favorite pizza or pie, you can easily see those chunks disappearing. Just having a clock nearby might help you stay on track.

# later, gator?

Do you put off anything that isn't due, like, tomorrow?
Take this quiz to figure out why.

**1.** Your book report is due on Monday. You . . .

   **a.** checked out a book but haven't started it yet. It looks so thick!

   **b.** will probably choose a book any day now. You don't like to rush into things.

**2.** Your friend asks, "What are you doing for your science project?" You say . . .

   **a.** "I don't know! I just can't think of anything. I'm starting to panic."

   **b.** "I dunno, but I'm sure my mom will help me. It'll be fun!"

**3.** You're not totally prepared for the math test tomorrow. So tonight, you're . . .

   **a.** staring at the ceiling, trying hard not to count sheep (because that reminds you of math and wigs you out).

   **b.** sleeping like a baby. You can study on the ride to school tomorrow.

**4.** History test. Tuesday. You got a bad grade on the last one, but you . . .

   **a.** can't seem to open your history book and study. Just looking at it makes you feel like you're coming down with the plague.

   **b.** shrug it off and tell yourself the last test was a fluke. You'll ace this one, no prob.

**5.** You're halfway done with your slideshow presentation, but before you move on, you . . .

   **a.** try to perfect those first few slides. Should the borders be lime green or greenish yellow? Hmm . . . you just can't decide.

   **b.** watch TV, play some games, and call a friend. Why rush? Everyone knows you work best under pressure.

## Answers

If you chose **mostly a's,** big projects and tests **overwhelm** you. You don't even know where to start! As the days tick on, that stress paralyzes you and keeps you from moving forward. It's not fun to feel that way, and it's hard to do your best work when you're hyperventilating. So tell yourself this: Big projects are just small projects strung together. If you shrink them down to size, you can more easily knock them off your list. Tests? Same thing. If you study a little every day, studying for tests will feel like regular homework—and a whole lot less scary.

If you chose **mostly b's,** you might be a little **overconfident** about what you can do in the time you have. Maybe you've pulled off last-minute studying before, but that doesn't mean it'll always work. What if you forget to bring a book home the night before a test? Or have technical difficulties with the computer? Or Mom has plans and can't help with your project (gasp!)? Even if you get it done, you're probably not doing your best work. If you can't work without a deadline staring you in the face, give yourself one. Break down projects into smaller chunks and set mini deadlines. Put them on your calendar and then knock them out, one by one.

# procrastination

Have you ever put off studying for a test, doing a big project, or something else important until the very last minute? If so, you're not alone! Here's what some girls have to say about procrastination—and how to beat it.

I had 3 whole weeks to do a science project. But suddenly it was the day before! I had to miss my gymnastics meet and recycling club to get it done, and it was so messy it did not deserve even the D it got. I will never wait till the last minute again!
—Leora

I had a science test the next day, but I plopped on the couch to watch TV. At the last minute I remembered, but I was sleepy so I read only one page. I made a really bad grade on the test. I was furious at myself!
—Hallie

DO NOT wait to study if you want a good grade!!!
—Rien

Once I had this really big exam coming up. The day before, I spent HOURS searching through my book for the answers. My mom helped me, but she was really annoyed.
—Nola

I put things off a lot so I am often in a hurry. One time I didn't look at a rubric for a project before I wrote a story. I didn't use any words I was supposed to use. My teacher said I wrote a good story but didn't do the project! Now I always check the rubric when I think I'm done.
—Annie

I put off reading my book for a book report, so I had to spend my whole weekend writing the report. I got a good grade, but I missed my weekend!
—AG Fan

Luckily, I've never had to do a big project at the last minute. I try to set aside an hour each day to study. I study for 15 minutes, followed by a 5-minute break, until my hour is up.
—Trina

# breaking it down

Whatever the reason for procrastinating on projects, the solution is the same: Break the project down into smaller steps. Imagine, for example, that you're planning a party. Make a list of the things you'd need to do to get that party off the ground. Maybe you would . . .

1. make a guest list
2. send out invitations

3. plan a menu
4. go shopping with a parent

5. clean your room
6. prep music and games

MENU

smoothies

mini sandwiches

veggie dip

cookies

7. make the food
8. greet your guests!

## Sounds fun, right?
And not too overwhelming!

That's something school projects and party planning have in common. If you break them down into smaller steps, they feel a lot more doable. Your school projects might not involve music and munchies (unless you get creative or have a super-cool teacher), but you can march your way through them, step by step, and come out on the other side.

Follow these tips to take the stress out of *any* project planning:

**Make a list.** Write out the steps you need to take.

**Set deadlines.** Work backward from the due date, figuring out how much time you need for each step. Then write those mini deadlines in your school planner or on a calendar.

**Reward yourself.** Give yourself a pat on the back for hitting deadlines. Or here's an idea: When you finish your project, plan a party!

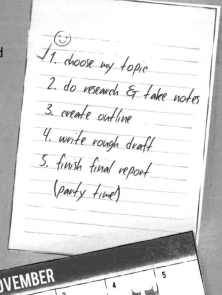

☺
✓1. choose my topic
2. do research & take notes
3. create outline
4. write rough draft
5. finish final report
   (party time!)

NOVEMBER

| 1 Topic | 2 | 3 | 4 | 5 |
| 8 | 9 research & notes | 10 | 11 Outline | 12 |
| research & notes 14 | 15 | 16 | 17 18 | 19 |
| 13 | 22 | Draft 23 | 24 25 | 26 |
| 20 21 FINAL hand in! | 28 | 29 30 | | |
| 27 | | | | |

## One small step

Just start. Set a timer for five minutes, and do the first step: Brainstorm topics for your project or report. Starting is the hardest part (honest!). Once you've done it, the next step will feel that much easier.

# tackling tests

You can try to cram all your studying into the night before the test, but your brain can hold only so much. Studying is like pouring a glass of root beer. If you pour in too much too fast, it'll fizz up and spill over the edge. Your brain won't be able to store the information—and a lot of panic and worry will come bubbling out. Don't do that to yourself! Instead, spread out your studying across time.

## A week before

Schedule study days. If the only deadline written in your planner is the day of the test, you'll see it on the horizon and think, "Hey, I've got plenty of time!" Don't let that deadline stand alone in your planner. Choose two or three other days when you can study during the week leading up to the test.

**What will you do on those days? Ask yourself these questions:**

- What will the test cover? How many pages or chapters?

- What books or notes do I need to bring home to study?

- How can I quiz myself? With flash cards? With practice tests?

- Who can help me study? (A parent? A sibling? A friend?)

Maybe on the first study night, you'll read a certain number of pages or make a set of flash cards. Maybe the next night, you'll ask Dad to quiz you. (Be sure to ask him ahead of time.) Whatever steps you choose, schedule them in your planner. Be specific. Write down exactly what you plan to do each day.

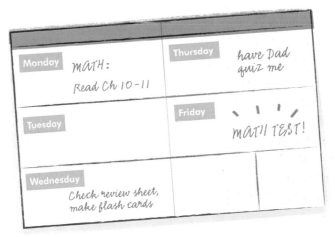

| Monday MATH: Read Ch 10-11 | Thursday have Dad quiz me |  |
| --- | --- | --- |
| Tuesday | Friday MATH TEST! |  |
| Wednesday Check review sheet, make flash cards |  |  |

# The night before

What's left to do? Nothing but one more review. Focus on the facts that tripped you up the most during the week. Then trust that you've done your best—because you have. You studied bit by bit and gave your brain time to soak up the material. Woo-hoo! Now you can make a root beer float and call it a night.

## One small step

Make the most of the time you have on test day. Read through the whole test as soon as you get it, guessing how much time each part might take. Answer the easy questions first, and then come back to the tougher ones. That way, you'll know exactly how much time you have left to spend on them.

# schedule smarts

# overscheduled?

You're juggling sports with school, and friends with family. Sometimes your calendar looks like an ink-pen explosion. Most of it is fun stuff, but how much is too much? Take this quiz to find out. Choose the answers that sound most like you.

**1.** Your friend Shelby wants you to try out for cheerleading, which meets Tuesday and Thursday afternoons. You have gymnastics on Tuesday and Thursday nights. You . . .

**a.** say no. You're flexible (you're a gymnast, after all), but your schedule on those days isn't—at least not right now.

**b.** tell Shelby you'll think about it. You might have to swap things around to make this work, but you've gotten pretty good at that.

**c.** say "Give me a Y. Give me an E. Give me an S. What's it spell? YES!" You always say yes—even when that little voice in your head says no.

**2.** Your piano teacher is sick, so you suddenly have a free hour to kill. You . . .

**a.** kick back and crack open that book you've been dying to read.

**b.** check your planner. There's probably something else you should be doing right now.

**c.** have absolutely no idea what to do with yourself. Should you call a friend? This downtime kind of freaks you out.

**3.** During a crazy-busy week when you're flying from one activity to the next, the thing that gets squeezed out is . . .

   **a.** free time. Every second of the day is planned. You make it through, but yikes, you could sure use a break.

   **b.** studying and practice time. You don't always get the best grades, and your piano teacher is less than impressed with your progress.

   **c.** sleep. It's the easiest thing to go, right? It is—until you're in school the next day and your teacher turns down the lights for a video. (Insert lullaby music here.)

**4.** At the start of a school day, the thing you look forward to most is . . .

   **a.** the bell ringing at the end of last period. That's when the fun part of your day begins.

   **b.** the moment when you're finally back at home, your homework is done, and you can r-e-l-a-x.

   **c.** bedtime. Can you just crawl back under the covers right now? You're already tired.

**5.** Uh-oh. Calendar crash. Your robotics club field trip is scheduled for this weekend. And you have to write your article for the school newspaper. And your friend just invited you to a sleepover. You . . .

   **a.** get creative. You invite your friend to stay at your house another night. And you write your newspaper article about robotics. Ta-da!

   **b.** know you can't do it all, but you sure want to. You ask your parents for help figuring out what to do.

   **c.** go to the sleepover and stay up way too late. You sleepwalk your way through the field trip. Then you go home and crash. (Newspaper article? What newspaper article?)

# Answers

If you chose **mostly a's,** you're a smart scheduler who knows her limits. You enjoy some after-school activities, but you protect your free time, too. You know how to say no, which means you have room in your schedule to say yes when you really want to. As you roll into high school and beyond, you'll have even more demands on your time, but you have the skills to navigate them. Keep doing what you're doing!

If you chose **mostly b's,** you're still in control of your schedule—but just barely. Maybe you enjoy being busy, or you even think you thrive on it. But make sure you know the warning signs of being overscheduled: trouble sleeping, slipping grades, and overall grumpiness. If you see the signs—or you find yourself having to turn down invitations for things you really want to do—it's time to take something out of your schedule. Create space for what matters most to you.

If you chose **mostly c's,** your schedule is careening out of control. You may love everything you're doing, but you've got way too much of a good thing going on. When that happens, there's no way to enjoy it all—or to do it well. Your sleep is probably suffering, and your grades may be, too. Take a step back and look at your schedule. Something's gotta give— maybe more than one "something." Figure out what can go, and then don't rush to fill that space.

# track it

Not sure where your time is going? Get it all on the calend
better yet, in a school planner or assignment notebook that breaks
down the hours in a day. Think about your schedule for the
next month, and follow these steps:

**Step 1:** Write down every sports practice, club meeting, recital, sleepover, and event. Sync up your planner with your family calendar to make sure you aren't forgetting anything.

**Step 2:** Block off time for homework, chores, getting cleaned up, and any other regular routines—including sleep!

**Step 3:** Flip through your planner and search for white space (the blanks in your planner where nothing is scheduled). How much do you see?

**MONDAY**

| | |
|---|---|
| 6:30 | Prep for day |
| 10:00 | Book Report D |
| 12:00 | Lunch ☺ |
| 4:00 | BB Practice |
| 5:30 | Dinner |
| 6:30 | Chores |
| 7:00 | Homework |
| 9:00 | Bedtime ☽ ✦ |

Some girls need lots of free time to recharge. Others need less. But every girl needs some. And it's easy to tell when you're not getting enough. You might have trouble sleeping or concentrating in school. Maybe you feel stressed out, cry easily, or have a short fuse with family and friends. Or you just feel tired—all the time. Sound familiar? Then it's time to free up some space in your schedule.

## One small step

Schedule some white space with your family. Challenge them to find an hour next weekend when no one plans anything—no homework, no chores, no sleepovers, no sports. What do you do with it? Give your brain time to be creative—or to power down for a while, if that's what your body is telling you it needs.

# what can go?

Take a look at your planner, and think about which activities are optional and which are not. Your parents may let you leave the drama club or switch from track to softball. But they probably won't let you skip the family reunion or church on Sundays. For every activity you do have a choice about, ask yourself these questions:

## Do I look forward to it?

Maybe you do—or you did when you started, but something's changed. Maybe you never really enjoyed it, but you've stuck it out because your parents or friends wanted you to. If you're dreading the activity, ask yourself how long you've felt that way—and why.

## Could I take a break from it and start again later?

Some things are easier to press "pause" on than others, like music lessons that you take on your own or babysitting. Team sports are a little tougher, but when the season ends, you always have the freedom and the choice to sit out the next season.

## Is there something else I'd rather do with that time?

It doesn't have to be another club or sport. It could be catching up on homework, or just getting more time to rest and recharge.

MONDAY

*Save time for homework*

TUESDAY

~~drama club~~

WEDNESDAY

*soccer practice (Keep for now)*

THURSDAY

FRIDAY

*babysit Nordskog twins*

SATURDAY

KEEP OPEN!

SUNDAY

Make a list of anything you don't enjoy, and think about why you're still doing it.

Is it a way to spend time with friends? Maybe there's something else you can do to get that time with them.

Is it because your parents want you to do it? Maybe it's time to talk with them about switching to a different sport, music, or volunteer activity— or about what else you'd like to do with the extra time (like sleep!).

I ♥ BAKING with FRIENDS

## One small step

If sorting through your schedule feels overwhelming, try this: Each time you rush off to another activity, draw an emoji or doodle in your planner to show how you're feeling. Don't want to go? Draw a frowny face. Excited about it? Dash off two smiley faces. Not sure? Draw a so-so face. After a few weeks, look back over your doodles. Is it easy to see what you enjoy and what you don't?

# how to quit

You've made up your mind about what has to go. Good for you! But hold on a sec before you announce your plans to the world. Here's how to make a graceful exit.

## Talk to your parents first.

Your parents may have reasons for wanting you to stick with an activity. Maybe they've already paid for a full season. Maybe they loved the activity when they were kids and they think it's good for you, too. Or maybe they worry that you quit things too quickly. (Ask yourself: "Are they right?") Here are some ways to start the conversation:

- "I've been so stressed out lately with homework, practice, and chores. I don't know how to get it all done, but I have an idea for how to find more time. Can I talk to you about it?" (Hint: Stress the "I want more time for homework and chores" part. Who can argue with that?)

- "I know you loved dance when you were my age, but I'm not sure it's for me. If you're going to pay for lessons, can it be for something I like better and think I'm good at? Like tennis, maybe?" (Hint: Stress the "I don't want to waste your hard-earned money" part. You may not get the answer you want, but you'll probably earn a smile.)

- "I've been in choir for a year now, but I don't like it as much as I thought I would. Could I try something else, like drama club? I might be able to use some of what I learned in choir, and I think I'd enjoy it more." (Hint: Stress the "choir hasn't been a waste of time" part. You can build on it!)

## Choose the best end date.

Pick a time that won't leave teammates or friends hanging. Don't leave before a big game, or before dance camp when you've already told your best friend you'd room with her. Finish out the season, or talk with your coach about a natural stopping point. Another reason to wait? Your feelings may change. You might master a new skill, or a friend may join the club and make it feel fun again. Give yourself time to be sure about your decision.

## Tell your coach or instructor.

Instead of begging your parents to call your coach, do it yourself. It doesn't have to be scary—you're not doing anything wrong. In fact, if you announce the decision, you'll look like a mature girl who knows her own mind. Practice ahead of time so that you can easily explain your feelings. Thank your coach or instructor for all you've learned from her, and wish her luck with the new season.

## Talk to your friends.

Does a club-mate or teammate worry that life won't be the same without you? Reassure her that you'll still spend time together, and then make it happen. Cheer her on at the next game or performance, or set aside a date on the calendar for just the two of you. Now that you've freed up some space in your schedule, spend it on the things and people you care about most.

# 10 ways to say no

You've cleared space in your calendar. Woo-hoo! Now resist the urge to fill it back up. The next time a friend asks you to join something new, flex your "no" muscle. It's a small word, but a powerful one. And there are many ways to say it. Try these:

## One small step

Say, "I have to check with my parents first." That will buy you time to think about it—and to practice saying NO if you need to.

# a new day

Taking control of your space and schedule takes time. So pat yourself on the back for any steps you make, no matter how small. Figure out which tips in this book work for you, and add them to your routine. Now that you know the basics for getting it together, you can experiment with your own ideas, too.

How do you know when you've really gotten it together? You'll feel it—that sense of calm when you wake up in the morning and go to bed at night, the pleasure when you walk into your room and see what matters most to you. You'll get along better with parents and teachers. You'll have more free time for yourself and for friends. In the mirror, you'll see more confident smiles and fewer worried frowns.

Will you ever feel stressed out again or find yourself in a room full of clutter? Sure. But it won't happen as often, and you'll know how to make your way out of it—how to take back your time and reclaim your space.

You're a girl who's got it together, and you're going to keep it that way.

It's a new day.

# How's it going?

Write to us and let us know your tips and tricks for taking charge of your time, your space, and your stuff. What advice do you have for girls like you? How has your life gotten better? We'd love to know.

**Write to**
***Getting It Together* Editor**
**American Girl**
**8400 Fairway Place**
**Middleton, WI 53562**

# Here are some other American Girl books you might like:

*Each sold separately. Find more books online at americangirl.com.*

Parents, request a FREE catalog at **americangirl.com/catalog.**
Sign up at **americangirl.com/email** to receive the latest news and exclusive offers.